REFLECTIONS AT HOME
The Morning
Star Series

REFLECTIONS AT HOME
The Morning
Star Series

Relevant Daily Scriptures For the Informed Christian

JANUARY WORKBOOK

CRYSTAL V. HENRY

authorHOUSE®

AuthorHouse™
1663 Liberty Drive
Bloomington, IN 47403
www.authorhouse.com
Phone: 1-800-839-8640

First published by AuthorHouse   12/02/2011

ISBN: 978-1-4678-7010-8 (sc)
ISBN: 978-1-4678-7013-9 (ebk)

Library of Congress Control Number: 2011960206

Printed in the United States of America

Any people depicted in stock imagery provided by Thinkstock are models, and such images are being used for illustrative purposes only.
Certain stock imagery © Thinkstock.

This book is printed on acid-free paper.

This workbook is dedicated to the late Rev. Frank B. Mitchell, Jr. who showed us how we should live.

REFLECTIONS AT HOME

PREFACE

We live in a society today where many parents are so busy trying to make ends meet financially, their children have become morally, spiritually, and emotionally bankrupt. Too often by the time a child reaches tenth grade, he has had his fill of being "bored" educationally. We allow teachers to teach the same material in the same manner as they have done for the past twenty years and somehow we are amazed that the students of today, with all of their electronic toys, are turned off by the beautifully written lesson plans of lethargy.

The workbook will enable parents and teachers alike to promote educational fun in the life of every child. It is designed mainly for high school students because that is where the drop-out problem occurs today in our schools, urban and suburban. This is a chance to bring the lessons of life in the Bible to those thirteen and beyond. The workbook is meant to be used as a supplement to Sunday School class; Home School; Catholic School or you may use it just as a means to seriously start reading the Bible for yourself. It is written in a format that any parent can feel comfortable "teaching". Read the scripture of the day first, and then read the focus verses of the day. Depending on the lesson, it may take more than a day to complete and that's great. I challenge students to have an opinion of what's going on in the world. Sometimes the understanding of the teen is so delusional or so insightful that you are literally left speechless, but that's an opportunity to discuss and add your mature insight. Give them something to think about. Don't just tell me what you think but why you think it. It is designed to make everyone think, research, discuss, and write to realize the full potential of all that God has given to them.

JANUARY 1ST

REFLECTIONS AT HOME
EXODUS 21: 12-26

PARENT: THE FIRST TEACHER

Many people have heard the scripture "an eye for an eye, a tooth for a tooth, but vengeance is mine," saith the Lord. However in Exodus, this rule was instituted as a guide for judges and parents, and not as a rule for personal relationships. When this was written, the punishment for various crimes was extremely cruel which may still exist in some countries today, such as stoning only the woman in adultery or cutting off the hand of a thief.

In Exodus, death was the punishment for cursing or attacking one's parents. As in this instance, the rule suggested that this would be too harsh a punishment.

Parents must make wise decisions in order for discipline to be effective. Likewise the classroom teacher. Too many times in education those who never taught in an urban high school are the ones who make the decisions on how to run a classroom. One cannot learn how to discipline effectively with only paper credentials at the end of her name. The best lesson plans mean very little if the teacher cannot control the class. Parents, take the time at least once every year to visit the classroom of every teacher on your child's roster. 'Too often, one's job becomes an excuse. It is a crime that most parents do not meet the teachers of their children in high school and the punishment is when they find out too late the child is not graduating which may have been prevented.

Ask God for wisdom.

JAPAN
CARD #1

JANUARY 2ND

REFLECTIONS AT HOME
JOB 3: 11-19

ACCEPTED AT THE KNEE

In many African nations when a baby is born, he is immediately placed on the knee of the father or mother. At this time, the child is "accepted" as their responsibility and their kin. Today there is an expectation in many young mothers for the government to feed, shelter, educate, and provide free childcare. The practice to accept immediate "ownership" of this little person has somehow gotten lost. The young father has already moved on to another lady in many cases, and the pride he has in creating children he has no intention of taking care of, is dysfunctional at best.

Is there any wonder why so many of our children regret having been born? Why type of home welcomed them? Did you read bedtime stories to them? Did you teach them social skills and manners. Did you check their homework at night? Were they left alone while you worked? Did you take them places to expose them to different cultures and customs? Do you take them to church?

The world will challenge your child. What have you instilled in them that will help them withstand adversity? Jesus is the rock. It is never too late to become a better parent.

Card #2

JANUARY 3RD

REFLECTIONS AT HOME
JOB 10: 13-22

"HAVE A LITTLE TALK WITH JESUS"

One of the worst things enacted when trouble comes along is to isolate oneself with the belief that no one else has similar problems. Self-condemnation and shame usually will keep the individual from receiving the help that is needed at this time, be it financial, heartache, or educational. Unfortunately, many families teach their children to be silent about family matters when if someone else had known about a problem, assistance could have prevented the festering before the tragic ending. Children learn how to handle problems by watching how their parents handle their problems: discussions, fighting, yelling, or pretending that there is no problem.

The key is not to be silent but one must talk to the right person when seeking help. When times are hard, the first one to talk with is Jesus. He can give you peace of mind over any earthly problem that is destroying your sleep. One's sounding board should not automatically be your best friend. If there is a problem in the marriage, perhaps one should not seek advice from someone who has never been married, nor advice from someone on a third marriage. There is no problem too small or too large that cannot be shared with Jesus.

Job says, "changes and war are ever with me." This may indicate that one is enveloped in self-pity or perhaps one's priorities need changing. Living in a constant state of high-alert can and will bring about health issues such as ulcers or high blood pressure. My mother used to say that "Everyone needs a reason to get up in the morning". This was her way of saying that if your whole life is centered on only you, this will lead to an empty life in the end. If you are lonely, don't settle for just anyone. Adopt a dog or cat. You will both benefit. If you are under fifty and alone, adopt a child. What greater gift can one give than to save a life?

Cajun-adopted
09-09-11

PLOT STRUCTURE

EXPOSITION — THE OPENING WHICH
INTRODUCES THE
CHARACTERS

COMPLICATION — THE MAIN CHARACTER TAKES
ACTION TO RESOLVE THE
CONFLICT

CLIMAX — WHEN EMOTIONS ARE THE
GREATEST

DENOUEMENT
OR RESOLUTION — WHEN THE STRUGGLES
ARE OVER AND A GRADUAL
BRINGING DOWN OF THE
CLIMAX

JANUARY 4TH

REFLECTIONS AT HOME
PLOT STRUCTURE

What happens when an eleven year-old is in the care of a parent who is mentally unstable?

PLOT STORY MAP

_____

CHARACTERS:

_____
_____
_____
_____

CONFLICT:
WHAT DO THE CHARACTERS WANT, AND WHAT PROBLEMS
DO THEY FACE?

_____
_____
_____
_____
_____

MAIN EVENTS:

1._____
2._____
3._____

DENOUEMENT:

_____
_____
_____
_____
_____

#1: Cheese store in South Philly

Talking Points:

1. "If you stay in it for any length of time, like anyplace else, a cafe becomes a world". (pg 5) Most urban high school students lack exposure beyond their own communities. What are the negatives and positives of one's whole world being a radius of less than 10 miles?

2. Clare says that her mother is a cross between a fairytale princess and an exotic animal like a peacock. Have each daughter tell what her mother is a cross between and the same for the mother telling about her mother (the grandmother). Are any surprised at the answers? Tell why they picked what they did for the comparisons.

3. Why is Cornelia surprised to discover that she is in love with Teo? Were you surprised? Why or why not? Is what ways is he exactly what she was looking for? In what ways is he not? What do you make of his relationship with Ollie? Do you think he and Cornelia have a chance? Why or why not?

#2: Rittenhouse Square at Christmastime

Talking Points:

1. Clare's friend, Josie, tells her that daughters aren't responsible for their mothers' behavior". Even though this may be true, how can a mothers' negative behavior affect the daughter in high school? What are some of the behaviors of the mother that may embarrass a daughter? (pg 61)

2. "I lived inside the four grim walls of my failure". (pg 92) Go around in a circle and let each mother and daughter state what that quote means to her. Is there any significance in the names of the women in this novel: Ollie? Audie? Linny? (Facilitator will read "A Dream Deferred" by Langston Hughes) Discuss the difference in missed opportunities and opportunities missed.

3. In the end, do you think Cornelia makes the right decision to leave Clare with Viviana? How is leaving them at Mrs. Goldberg's different than them returning to their own home? Why does it seem safer to all of them? Do you think Clare will really forgive Cornelia for leaving her?

#3: Café Dora

Talking Points:

1. "When I say I'm a coffee-bar manager, instantly everyone around me just thinks I'm an under-achiever". Do you believe that society judges one based on her occupation? How is this connected to self-worth? Why are so many high school students perceived as under-achievers today? What practical changes should be made? (pg 137)

2. Shakespeare and Santos talk about a "sea change", the alteration of one's life into something rich and strange. (pg 210) Daughters tell your mothers what college you plan on attending and how it will change your life. Mothers of experience, tell your daughters about a "sea change" in your life they perhaps do not know about.

3. What does Mrs. Goldberg represent to Cornelia? How do her memories of Mrs. Goldberg help her through difficult situations? How do her stories about Mrs. Goldberg help Clare? What does Goldberg's house represent to Cornelia? To Clare? Why does Clare want so badly to stay there? Daughters tell what your house represents to you and why.

JANUARY 5TH

REFLECTIONS AT HOME
ISAIAH 44: 1-5

TO POUR: TO CAUSE TO FLOW IN A STEADY STREAM

We live in a time when civil rights seem to be going back to a time of shame for the United States. The outwardly, in your face, arrogant racists have taken off their sheets for the world to see. Sadly, misguided, people have placed these instruments of Hell into the orchestra of the Congress. There has been a steady stream of hate since the election of the first Black President, Barack Obama.

How do you fight this abhorrent, peculiar institution? By letting everyone know about your relationship with Christ by the way you live. "For I will pour water upon Him that is thirsty, and floods upon the dry ground: I will pour my spirit upon thy seed . . ." When Gwendolyn Foster, a gifted vocalist, would sing, "Ho, Everyone That Thirsteth", and hold that high note, it brought tears to my eyes and made my heart feel like it was about to burst. Christ is the Living Water. When the world seems crazy, remember the life-giving power of water not only for your sake, but for the sake of your children.

During the time of slavery, it was a common practice to brand the back of the slave's hand to indicate who owned him. "One shall say, I am the Lord's . . . and another shall subscribe with his hand unto the Lord . . . (verse 5). The world should know that you are a child of God and belong to him. As parents and churches, we must teach our "seed" the lessons of the Bible to increase their understanding, knowledge, and wisdom.

When we visited Egypt, we spent time in a Nubian Village where they painted the hands of the women and the arms of the men in an effort to share their culture. This presents an excellent and fun way to learn about religious symbols such as the peacock, the symbol for immortality or the butterfly, the symbol for the resurrection. A henna/mehndi artist can be invited to attend a church fair or a party in your home and paint the Christian symbol of your choice on the back of your hand signifying that you are owned by God. Make the Bible relevant to your children until their knowledge flows like a steady stream.

EGYPT

Card #3

JANUARY 6TH

REFLECTIONS AT HOME
JEREMIAH 20: 10-18

MOOD SWINGS

Whenever someone sets out to defame someone else by attacking his good name or reputation, look to see what he expects to gain from it. Just as Jeremiah was compelled to share the word about Christ because it was like "fire within his bones", he was ridiculed, had an unpopular ministry, and put in stocks. Unlike the so-called friends of Jeremiah, as Christians we should not be a silent crowd when an injustice has occurred. Ignorance is not a character trait one should strive for as a Christian. Today's person of faith must be informed, intelligent, and take action at the ballot box to remove the hate-filled, racists from office. Do what you can and trust God to take care of the rest.

"But the Lord is with me as a mighty, terrible one:
Therefore my persecutors shall stumble, and they shall not prevail:
They shall be greatly ashamed; for they shall not prosper:
Their everlasting confusion shall never be forgotten."

Jeremiah 20: 11

Like Jeremiah, feel the injustice as if it was "fire in your bones" and help get out the vote. Take a friend to get a driver's license or a state photo I.D. card. They are counting on you not having "your papers"!

JANUARY 7TH

REFLECTIONS AT HOME
PSALM 139: 13-24

ALWAYS

Morning Prayer: Search me, O God, and know my heart:
Try me, and know my thoughts:
And see if there be any wicked way in me,
And lead me in the way everlasting
Verses 23, 24

It is very comforting to be loved. God tells us to have respect for ourselves and realize that because we are wonderfully-made, we cannot be worthless. God expects loyalty to Him as one would expect loyalty from a spouse. He is always near and therefore we must constantly search our hearts and be aware not to act in a manner based on wrong motives. Many times couples will have a special sentiment written on the inside of their wedding rings to remind each other of their enduring affection over a lifetime. You must belong to Christ for a lifetime.

Some people have a habit of saying exactly the opposite of what is in their hearts and then try to justify the act if caught: cheating on one's spouse, participating in inhumane animal cruelty, lying about someone for personal gain. Too often these actions are sanctioned by society with the excuse that "Everyone does it". As Christians, we cannot and should not turn a blind eye. Without being didactic or condescending, anywhere we see injustice being done, ask God to lead them in the way everlasting.

HAWAII
CARD #4

JANUARY 8TH

REFLECTIONS AT HOME
ECCLESIASTES 11: 1-6

WAITING FOR GODOT

To The Graduates Everywhere:

As you begin the next phase of life leaving the safe cocoon of your parents, understand that life involves both risk and opportunity. If you want to find the perfect college, you won't go beyond a high school diploma; if you want to find the perfect church, you will never join; if you search for the perfect ministry, you will never serve. To be a diligent or assiduous person, one must be a hard-working individual, not someone who just shows up for work and leaves at the end of the day. It's the person who is always trying to improve the way something is done by asking questions; offering solutions; and is cognizant of how others before them have achieved success.

"Cast thy bread upon the waters: for thou shalt find it after many days . . .

Give a portion to seven or eight . . ."

11: 1,2

To be diligent also means to be careful and steady. In Biblical times when the weather was not predicted as it is today, one would send grain on seven or eight different trading ships in case the weather capsized one of the ships. Today we say "Don't put all of your eggs in one basket". With your college degree in hand, and with the acceptance of your new job—from the very first paycheck, diversify!

1. Set up a 40lK or ROTH IRA tax advantaged account
2. Set up an automatic deposit authorization
3. Allocate 10% of your take home pay to stocks or stock mutual funds
4. Allocate 10% of your take home pay to bonds
5. Allocate 10% to your church
6. Allocate 10% to savings for that down payment towards home ownership
7. Plan an annual vacation somewhere that does not include just visiting relatives

"In the morning sow thy seed . . ."

11: 6

Build your foundation in the time of your youth.

CARD #5

JANUARY 9TH

REFLECTIONS AT HOME
DANIEL 9: 20-27

WHISPER A PRAYER IN THE EVENING

Have you ever prayed for something, and then surprised when your prayers were answered? When Daniel prayed, the Lord sent his messenger, Gabriel, to talk with Daniel. He told Daniel that "I am now come forth to give thee skill and understanding." When your prayers have been answered, were they answered in the way you expected? At certain times in your life God places people, who at first may not seem that significant, but in time become your "rock in a weary land." There was once a Jewish slave girl named Esther who was taken from her home and married a king, saving her people from massacre; not unlike David, a shepherd boy, who became king. Watch the movie, "One Night With The King" starring Tiffany DuPont as Queen Esther for family enjoyment.

The foreign ruler alluded to in verse 26 was Antiochus IV who outlawed Jewish religious rites and traditions and instead ordered the Jews to worship the Greek god, Zeus. When strangers come into your life and turn it upside down, be it at your job or home, the Lord says that if you listen, he will give you the skill to triumph over adversity. How many people have had to endure a boss on the job who knew less about the job than they did, or an individual who tries to be your friend so he/she can get closer to your significant other? The Lord says that He decides the time when He destroys the one who destroys. It's not up to you. You must have the skill to recognize a snake when you see one and not be ruled by it. It's called discernment.

In verse 26, it tells of how the Messiah will be rejected and killed by His own people. Gabriel came to also give understanding. It's hard when one tries to cope with betrayal by friends and family. Your friends and family know your strengths and weaknesses best. Understand that Christ endured the ultimate betrayal and that you cannot wallow in self-pity or waste seventy weeks or seventy days. Many times when we take the blinders off or our eyes, the understanding of an act of betrayal was there all along.

Find a new purpose in your life. Make a commitment to help someone or something else for seventy weeks as your personal offering or your "evening oblation."

JAPAN
CARD #6

ALLUSION

A REFERENCE TO A FAMOUS
PERSON, EVENT IN HISTORY,
OR THE BIBLE

JANUARY 10TH

REFLECTIONS AT HOME
DANIEL 12: 1-13

A VISION

A vision is the power of perceiving by clear thinking while awake. When someone has a vision, it not only involves sight, but a desire to understand what one has witnessed. We see men today foolishly trying to predict the end of time based on calculations. Every time they are wrong, it should break their pride and air of self-sufficiency. No man can predict when it is your turn to "sleep in the dust of the earth". Likewise, one cannot understand the exact meanings and events in a vision for God has said many times in the Bible that everything will not be revealed to us in this life. This is known as stepping out on faith.

A vision never leaves you. At times, it can be all-consuming. One may question whether or not he should share his vision with others for fear of being thought crazy or a fanatic. The Lord is very much alive today and to think that only the prophets of the Bible received visions and somehow God just stopped "talking" to mankind two thousand years ago is illogical for a Christian. God is the Alpha and the Omega.

". . . and they that turn many to righteousness as the stars forever and ever"

12: 3

I want you to think about two men who had similar visions. While exiled on the island of Patmos in the Aegean Sea, Jesus spoke to John in a vision whereby John wrote the Book of Revelation based on his vision.

For those who do not subscribe to the New Testament or the belief that it was truly the Son of Man, Jesus, who hung on the cross atop Golgotha, I refer you to the vision of Daniel given to him by the guardian angel, Michael, in the Old Testament.

*As a family, watch the movie "the Book of Eli" starring Denzel Washington and then fill out the Venn diagram on the next page comparing and contrasting Eli to John. If you have already seen the movie, I think your "vision" of the movie will be enhanced in a new way.

BUT THOU, O DANIEL, SHUT UP THE WORDS, AND SEAL THE BOOK, EVEN TO THE TIME OF THE END . . . DANIEL 12:4

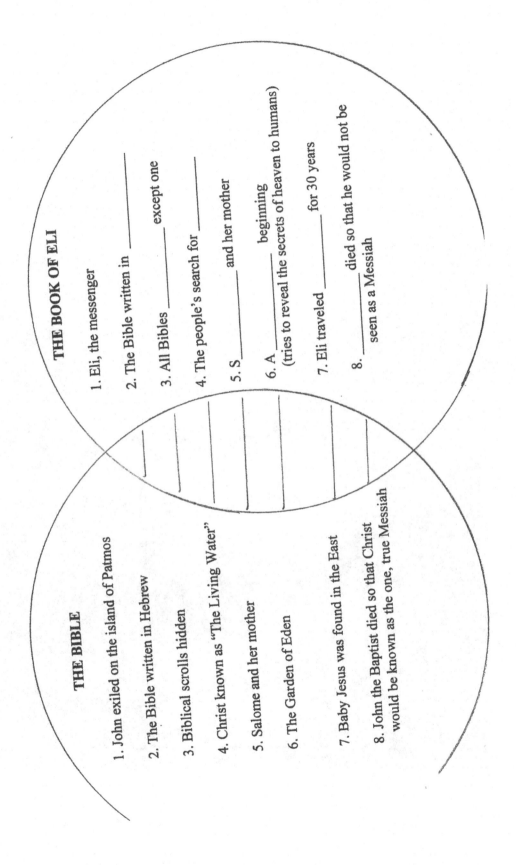

THE BOOK OF ELI

1. Eli, the messenger

2. The Bible written in _____ except one

3. All Bibles _____

4. The people's search for _____

5. S _____ and her mother

6. A _____ beginning (tries to reveal the secrets of heaven to humans)

7. Eli traveled _____ for 30 years

8. _____ died so that he would not be seen as a Messiah

THE BIBLE

1. John exiled on the island of Patmos

2. The Bible written in Hebrew

3. Biblical scrolls hidden

4. Christ known as "The Living Water"

5. Salome and her mother

6. The Garden of Eden

7. Baby Jesus was found in the East

8. John the Baptist died so that Christ would be known as the one, true Messiah

33

JANUARY 11TH

REFLECTIONS AT HOME
MATTHEW 13: 15-28

DOUBLE MEANINGS

Abominations are anything that arouse strong disgust or loathing, but Jesus taught about the "abomination of desolation" on the Mount of Olives. These abominations were events that mocked Him such as when Antiochus IV Epiphanes sacrificed a pig to Zeus on the sacred temple altar or false prophets whose "lying lips are abomination to the Lord" (Proverbs 12:22). Unless you have a strong foundation of understanding of God's word, you will not be able to perceive distortions when you hear them. In the *Narrative in the Life of Frederick Douglass* he states that the preachers were the most violent, hate-filled slave owners around.

"Men never do evil so completely and cheerfully as when they do it from religious conviction." (Blaise Pascal)

Jesus teaches that you will not need to be told that He has returned when He does return. You will know Him and see Him for yourself.

"For as the lightning cometh out of the East, and shineth even unto the West: so shall also the coming of the son of man be" (Matthew 24:27)

Jesus also teaches us not to have a mob mentality. It still amazes me after twenty-five years of teaching how in some high schools if someone yells fight", all of the kids come running to see the "show". Because Christ took on the form of humanity, He understood our abominable behavior.

"For wheresoever the carcase is, there will be the eagles/buzzards gathered together" (24:28)

Some Bibles say eagles, some use the word buzzards. The eagle was the symbol of the Roman army which could refer to the Roman occupation and the many who died under their oppression. The "buzzards" of today gather around and stare when anything bad happens, often not even lifting a finger to help because we find it entertaining to see suffering or we don't want to get involved.

Hanukkah Festival was the rededication of the Jewish temple in Jerusalem three years after the acts of Antiochus and the victory in 165 BC by the Macabees over the Syrians. What abominations exist in your life? Ask your children how do they respond when they hear the word "fight" in school. Do they run towards it or away from it?

ASHEVILLE, N. CAROLINA
SMOKY MTS.
CARD #7

JANUARY 12TH

REFLECTIONS AT HOME
MARK 13: 14-23

THE REDEMPTIVE PRIESTS

If you call yourself a Christian and have lived a little while, there probably have been times when what someone meant for evil upon you, was changed to good by God.

The 'abomination of desolation" referred to several times in the Bible is the desecration of the sacred temple. However, desecration may come in many forms. As discussed in Matthew 24 when Antiochus sacrificed a pig to Zeus on the sacred temple altar, or when Nebuchadnezzar looted the temple and took Judean captives to Babylon in 597 BC.

> ". . . let them that be in Judea flee to the mountains"
> (Verse 14)

Pedophiles in the priesthood have been a looming problem for centuries, but with money, all things can be hidden for a while. I believe that a deceiving Christian is one who promotes hostility towards other Christians. The problem has long been documented and in a sense, the crime can never be repaid, however I think that instead of putting the offenders in jail where they will receive three meals a day and television, create a new "order" whereby they have to wear a scarlet "R" on their clothing for seven years.

During these seven years, the "Redemptive Order" would be forced to revisit the vows of poverty and self-sacrifice, and follow the concepts of

St. Gregory I, The Great who was consumed with missionary activities as well as the creator of the Gregorian Chant.

In tribes of twelve each, these convicted redemptive priests would be guarded and assigned to manual labor (not near any children) from 9-5 in the Republic of Burundi; the Democratic Republic of the Congo; and the Republic of Haiti. (Even though President Obama requested $100,000. to assist Haiti, the current Republican Congress denied the funding nine times.) These three places are some of the most impoverished places on Earth. The priests may even learn a new language like Kirundi.

They stole the childhood of many from their high perch on the altar.

JANUARY 13TH

REFLECTIONS AT HOME
AMOS 1: 1-15

THE FIG TREE

Since the time of Adam and Eve, the fig tree has played a prominent role. It provides food, shade, and sometimes serves as a piece of clothing. Today we readily buy Fig Newtons for our little ones and if money allows, we can make prosciutto wrapped figs for the adults as a special treat. However, the ordinary looking fig is brownish green on the outside while encasing a beautiful pink, sweet inside.

This reminded me of how God uses ordinary people to accomplish extraordinary things. An ordinary farmer who tended his sheep and sycamore fig trees was chosen to leave his farm in the southern kingdom of Judah and travel to the northern kingdom of Israel to warn about the impending judgement on the nations' wealthy people who were oppressing the poor.

As a Christian, your lifestyle should reflect your devotion. Amos spoke against those who ignored the needy after the Lord had blessed them so tremendously. God calls on all Christians to work against the injustices in society. Although today we find many millionaires, I call on two who have jobs that represent the people of the United States, one of Lebanese immigrant parents and the other with Austro-Hungarian roots.

In spite of dropping out of high school and having many dubious incidents with stolen cars, weapons, and insurance fraud, Congressman Darrell Issa became the Chairman of the Committee on Oversight and Government Reform and is financially worth $452 million dollars according to personal finance disclosure. As an Antiochian Orthodox

Christian, the people of Allen, South Dakota need his help. Maybe Congressman Issa can build a Health Science Community College where all of the residents of ten years attend free.

Congressman John Kerry, of the Roman Catholic faith, earned the silver star, the bronze star, and three purple and is financially worth $295 million dollars. He is the Chairman of the Committee on Foreign Relations but the people of Cuevitas, Texas could use his help. Perhaps Kerry could build a Criminal Justice Community College where all of the residents of ten years attend free.

Like Amos, I know that you can't control someone else's money but think of the good it would do in Allen and Cuevitas. Remember the fig tree. Have a sweet inside.

EGYPT
CARD #8

JANUARY 14TH

REFLECTIONS AT HOME
EZEKIEL 16: 15-30

APOSTASY

(Spiritual Adultery; Turning from God)

When I read this passage, it reminded me so much of the book, *Madam Bovary* by G. Flaubert. Unlike a few decades ago, the people of today are more of a visual type of learner. Endowing the abstract by using personification sometimes does not have the full impact of what has just been written. So, I am presenting a comparison of the likes of Madame Bovary to Jerusalem's harlotry. Give an example from the novel of each of her traits.

After you have read the novel, then watch the 1949 version of Madame Bovary starring Jennifer Jones (found on amazon.com). She truly captures the desperation of a deceitful life and the ultimate dangerous demise leading to her death. Depending on which version you see, the ending concerning her daughter varies. However, this is in itself insignificant. The focus is M. Bovary.

Ezekiel 16: 15-30	*Madame Bovary*
1. Apostasy	1. Carnal adultery
2. Child sacrifice is forbidden	2. Child neglected
3. Dangerous pride	3. Destructive pride
4. Foolish vanity	4. Excessive vanity
5. Rebellion against God	5. Turned from God

6. Forgetting His help

7. Built shrines & idols to honor

8. Jerusalem "prostitutes" herself having sex with foreign nations & their gods

6. Using people as a means to an end

7. Worshiped fine clothes, jewelry,

8. Becomes a prostitute

Every teenage girl should see this movie. A certain lifestyle which may look glamorous is a ruse. Superficial values are bombarded into their heads making it harder for children to remember the teachings of home and church. Once again, the parents are a child's first teachers.

LOOK . . . . SEE . . . . LEARN

WHAT MATTERS IS NOT SO MUCH THE
CIRCUMSTANCES OF LIFE, BUT YOUR
RESPONSE TO THEM.

GENESIS 37:28

HAWAII
CARD #9

JANUARY 15TH

REFLECTIONS AT HOME
AMOS 6: 1-14

HOME ECONOMICS

I remember how horrified I was to find out that the Red Cross, a non-profit organization, was paying Elizabeth Dole $300,000. as President. Being a millionaire in her own right made the insult even worse. Why not pay her minimum wage since the persona was about the altruistic work she was doing?

Amos talks about how those who live in great mansions, displaying their wealth and comfortable lifestyles, are really isolated from the needs of others—in it but not of it. So many times the rich give fancy parties and programs to help the poor—when all they have to do is build something themselves. I recall Congresswoman Jane Harman, who resigned from the House to become the president of the Woodrow Wilson International Center for Scholars in Washington, D.C. I am reminded of her because of a quote she made in the 1998 gubernatorial race that she was "the best Republican in the Democratic race." She is said to be worth $435 million dollars or as one used to say, she is of "substance". The Center has very interesting lectures on many subjects, but are they providing any scholarships to Smith College (the alma mater of Harman) or Howard University for example?

When the poor are invisible, Amos says that the rich "cause the seat of violence to come near; that lie upon beds of ivory . . ." (6: 3, 4) One by one, we can eradicate poverty, not by simply writing checks, but by building dreams. Brundage, Texas is only one place out of many which could use some rebuilding. Ms. Harman and other millionaires could make a big difference in so many lives by providing at least one home for twelve families each who are currently living in homeless shelters all over this wonderfully, blessed nation.

What resources in your daily life are you wasting that someone less fortunate could use? One cannot succeed when the road is rocky. To run and win the race, there needs to be a smooth, even playing field. Perhaps your church can take one family out of a shelter and place them in a home as an annual project.

"Every time you reach out and touch a heart or a life, the world changes."
from *The Shack*
by Wm. Paul Young

**JAPAN
CARD #10**

JAMES WELDON JOHNSON

(1871-1938)

After reading the novel, *The Shack*, read this poem aloud at least twice and then write what you believe it is saying. How does "The Black Mammy" relate to *The Shack*? Go beyond the obvious color of her skin and define her traits that make her a refuge for lost souls.

Title: The Black Mammy

Author: James Weldon Johnson

O whitened head entwined in turban gay,
O kind black face, O crude, but tender hand,
O foster-mother in whose arms there lay
The race whose sons are masters of the land!
It was thine arms that sheltered in their fold,
It was thine eyes that followed through the length
Of infant days these sons. In times of old
It was thy breast that nourished them to strength
So often hast thou to thy bosom pressed
The golden head, the face and brow of snow;
So often has it 'gainst thy broad, dark breast
Lain, set off like a quickened cameo.
Thou simple soul, as cuddling down that babe
With thy sweet croon, so plaintive and so wild,
Came ne'er the thought to thee, swift like a stab,
That it some day might crush thine own black child?.

Although God the Father and God the Son are
equal, each has special work to do.

1Corinthians 15: 25-28

SITUATIONAL IRONY

THIS OCCURS WHEN THERE IS A CONTRAST BETWEEN WHAT WOULD SEEM APPROPRIATE AND WHAT REALLY HAPPENS.

Research "the Red Summer of 1919" in Chicago. This is a picture of what was going on during that time in history. Then look at the last line of the poem by James W. Weldon, "the Black Mammy", which was written in 1917. On the next page, explain the situational irony of the last line of the poem and how it connects to this picture.

SITUATIONAL IRONY IN
THE SHACK & "THE BLACK MAMMY"

*Write a paragraph (5 sentences) about each piece of literature explaining the situational irony in both.

_____

_____

_____

_____

_____

_____

_____

_____

_____

_____

_____

_____

_____

_____

_____

_____

_____

_____

_____

_____

JANUARY 16TH

REFLECTIONS AT HOME
JEREMIAH 3: 1-5

POLLUTING THE LAND

In this analogy a divorced woman symbolizes a nation who has divorced itself from the teachings of Moses also found in Deuteronomy 24. I want you to focus today on a telegram sent by General Miles on December 19, 1890.

General Miles' Telegram

General Miles sent this telegram from Rapid City to General John Schofield in Washington, D.C. on December 19, 1890:

Nelson A. Miles

"The difficult Indian problem cannot be solved permanently at this end of the line. It requires the fulfillment of Congress of the treaty obligations that the Indians were entreated and coerced into signing. They signed away a valuable portion of their reservation, and it is not occupied by white people, for which they have received nothing.

They understood that ample provision would be made for their support; instead, their supplies have been reduced, and much of the time they have been living on half and two-thirds rations. Their crops, as well as the crops of the white people, for two years have been almost total failures.

The dissatisfaction is wide spread, especially among the Sioux, while the Cheyennes have been on the verge of starvation, and were forced to commit depredations to sustain life. These facts are beyond question, and the evidence is positive and sustained by thousands of witnesses."

Ten days later, the response from the American government was the infamous massacre at Wounded Knee Creek in South Dakota. Some three hundred men, women, and children were mowed down by the Cavalry using Hotchkiss guns which looks like a cross between a repeating rifle and a canon. For this "act of bravery", the army awarded twenty medals of honor.

Today we have politicians who want to rewrite history due to their own lack of knowledge, their abhorrent apathy to even try to learn the history of this great country, and those who just make up their own version of history—you know how the Founding Fathers "worked tirelessly to end slavery" when every single one of them owned slaves except for John Adams, the second president (not to be confused with the son, John Quincy Adams, our sixth president). John Adams spent very little time at home, and did not need slaves. His wife Abigail wrote volumes of letters to him throughout the years which can now be found in any library.

". . . Thou hast polluted the land with thy whoredoms and wickedness . . .

Thou refusedst to be ashamed"

(3: 2, 3)

These actions of abomination are serious offenses against God. Instead of acknowledging past mistakes, those in power downplay the mistakes to relieve the guilt of the atrocities committed in the past. Lies lead to more lies.

God says in verse 1, "Why should I take you back?", after you have lied and committed offenses against His teaching.

Because He always gives us a second change to get it right. As in previous days, we call on another millionaire public servant, Senator

Mark Warner of Virginia. We know that education is the key to escape poverty, so think how wonderful it would be if Senator Warner could use his money to build a community college for Web Graphic Design in Wounded Knee, South Dakota and, as before, residents of ten years or more attend free. Stock its library with copies of *Bury My Heart At Wounded Knee* by Dee Brown and make it mandatory reading.

Three Medals of Honor were awarded among the 64,000 South Dakotians in World War II some fifty years after the massacre.

JANUARY 17TH

REFLECTIONS AT HOME
AMOS 9: 1-4

HIDING

"Though they dig into Hell, thence shall mine hand take them
Though they climb up to heaven, will I bring them down"

(9: 2)

Amos envisioned the Lord standing by the Temple altar in judgement. But, unlike God we often do not know what has influenced people's behavior. During the Civil War, there was a major in the U.S. Army named Edmund Smith from Florida. He was placed in military boarding school at the age of twelve where he learned to be a masterful leader. But in 1861, Major Smith resigned his commission in the U.S. Army to join the Confederacy taking his personal valet, a slave by the name of Alexander Darnes, with him. You see, the parents of Edmund owned slaves while he was fighting against slavery.

At the end of the Civil War, Smith fled to Mexico and then to Cuba to escape charges of treason. He hid from June to November until he was allowed to take the oath of amnesty at Lynchburg, Virginia.

What are you "hiding" from God? Family secrets? Financial secrets? Hiding is hard work and causes stress. Most people cannot hide how they were raised forever. It eventually slips out in one form or another. Today many people want to whitewash America's past and change the wording in Tom Sawyers' *Huckleberry Finn* for fear of offending people. His parents, like the parents of Smith, owned slaves so it is perfectly understandable why some degrading terms are used when addressing

Blacks in the novel. To change the words is to change history which I feel is dangerous. Words contain power.

The Lord says that He will find you wherever you may try to hide. But, just as Edmund Smith received amnesty, so shall you if you only ask.

Smith's personal valet, Alexander H. Darnes, went on to attend Lincoln University after 1865 and then on to Howard University school of medicine graduating from there in 1880. He became the first Black physician in the city of Jacksonville, Florida.

JANUARY 18TH

REFLECTIONS AT HOME
PROVERBS 28: 1-14

HOLLOW SELF-ESTEEM

"Evil men understand not judgement: but they that seek the Lord
understand all things."

(28: 5)

What are the qualifications to be President of the United States? Do
you know? Should the person not be able to tell hateful lies? Should we
expect the person to be courteous? Should there be a basic understanding
of facts as opposed to fiction regarding American history? Is it okay to be
a whoremonger? Should the person believe in some entity greater than
himself or herself? What color skin should he have? Should he look like
you? Are you one of the many "upset" people who read *The Shack* by
Young only to find out the God appeared to the guilt-ridden, distraught
father in the form of a comforting, motherly Black woman?

One of the first Black runway models in NY, Elaine Ellis, said that
she could work about ten years longer than her Caucasian colleagues due
to the melon in Black skin that helps to prevent wrinkles. Get a map of
the world and find the equator. When traveling in Egypt and beyond,
there was no one who had the lavender eyes and pale skin of Elizabeth
Taylor (Hollywood Cleopatra), nor did anyone resemble the blue eyes
and pale skin of Jeffrey Hunter (Hollywood Jesus). Yet good Christians
hold degrading signs and teach their innocent children their hatred for
people who do not look like them.

The One who is called the Alpha and the Omega can appear in any form. But in whatever form He decides to return, we will all be judged for how we have treated our fellow man.

". . . But by a man of understanding and knowledge The state thereof shall be prolonged."

(28: 2)

EGYPTIAN
BOYS

JANUARY 19TH

REFLECTIONS AT HOME
DEUTERONOMY 7: 16-26

"IS THERE ANY WORD FROM THE LORD?
LISTEN . . . LISTEN . . . LISTEN"
Allen W. Foster

I believe that if we listen to God's word, it teaches us how to live. The problem is that not everyone who carries the Bible, reads the Bible. Sure, many turn to the scripture during church service, but that is the only time during the week that book is opened. I wrote *Reflections At Home* because I want to show how relevant the Bible is today, just as it was for our grandparents.

Every so often, you should do a self-check. At _____ (age), I should be here in life and here is where I am now. Too many people wander aimlessly in life having no plans or obtainable goals and wonder why they haven't achieved much even though they are always busy. Everyone must have some organization to her life even though it sounds wonderful to be thought of as a free spirit. After a certain age, you are thought of as a hot mess—not dependable, always broke, and your word means nothing.

In Deuteronomy, Moses says remember what God did to Pharaoh. If you are obedient to God's word and try to live your life accordingly, God will bring you to a spiritual maturity and understanding step-by-step. The Lord will fight our battles whether it be on the job or with your teenage son or daughter. But, He will do it a little at a time so that you can handle the results. Not until you have been passed over on the job for that promotion several times will you finally take charge of your situation and send your resume elsewhere, but what did you learn those times of rejection? God gave you patience, diligence, and self-worth. With every stumbling block, He was getting you ready even though you thought you were ready years ago. Great lesson plans do not guarantee a great teacher. "Seasoned" teachers have a dimension to their lessons that new teachers do not possess no matter what university degree they possess.

"The graven images of their gods shall ye burn with fire: Thou shalt not desire the silver or gold that is on them, nor take unto thee, lest thou be snared therein . . ." (7: 25)

Take an assessment of your life; set some new goals; and do not envy those who may seem to have more than you. The Lord will bring you out one step at a time.

JAPAN

JANUARY 20TH

REFLECTIONS AT HOME
PROVERBS 6: 12-19

WICKED

In Proverbs 6, the Bible tells us that there are six things the Lord hates:

1. Pride
2. A lying tongue
3. Hands that shed innocent blood
4. A heart that devises wicked plans
5. Feet that are swift in running to evil
6. Those who stir up trouble in a family

Every year I cringe when it is my turn for jury duty. For me, it is very tedious because of the redundancy of the lawyers. But, the last murder trial I sat in on, I was surprised to see that the gang members of the people on trial were allowed to sit in the courtroom thumping their chests and making all kinds of gestures.

Since we did not know what they were communicating to each other, it was very intimidating for many. All one can do is not be dazzled by the attorneys and use your common sense for the most part to connect the dots.

"... a wicked man walketh with a froward mouth. He winketh with his eyes, he speaketh with his feet, he teacheth with his fingers."

(6: 12 & 13)

Do any of these traits have your name on them?

HAWAII
CARD # 11

JANUARY 21ST

REFLECTIONS AT HOME
PROVERBS 6: 12-19

PANFILO DeNARVAEZ

When Columbus was sailing the ocean blue, there was a certain man by the name DeNarvaez born in Spain. DeNarvaez grew up to become what our whitewashed textbooks would call a great explorer. In truth, he was known for the abhorrent violence on his ships. In 1526 the Holy Roman Emperor, Charles V, granted him the unexplored land of Florida to "colonize". (Growing up, I could never understand how someone could give someone else's land and home away without so much as a yawn.) Being no more than a hired mercenary, he would cut off the nose of the poor Indian who could not tell him where vast amounts of gold and silver could be found. He left Spain with some three hundred men picking up slaves all along his route past northern Africa.

"Therefore shall his calamity come suddenly;
Suddenly shall he be broken without remedy" (6: 15)

On his last voyage, DeNarvaez and his crew of three hundred were drowned in the ocean except for four men. One of the four was named Estevanico, a slave captured from Morocco. If you are interested in the real history of America, take the time to research what was left out of your school textbook. You may have a new appreciation for history.

Indian Freedom
The Cause of Bartolome De Las Casas
1484-1566
    By Francis P. Sullivan
(Chapter 3 tells the exploits of Panfilo DeNarvaez)

JAPAN

JANUARY 22ND

REFLECTIONS AT HOME
LUKE 16: 1-13

JOB CREATORS?

Money allows one to be powerful. It is up to us to use our financial gifts wisely and not selfishly squander them. One of our representatives, Congressman Jarid Polis of Colorado, has lived his life as a true philanthropist. From the beginning, he has shown a heart that truly speaks to the lifestyle mentioned in the book of Luke. We live in a time where all we are hearing from the Right Wing is how we can't tax the wealthy because they are the job creators. Polis had done this. What about Issa, Harman, Kerry, and Warner? Can you find how they have used their millions to put others to work?

Congressman Polis has already demonstrated his generosity, unlike the dishonest man in Luke who made sure that he looked out for himself better than he cared for his fellow man. The dishonest accountant did not see the needs of the "children of light" (Romans 12). He only saw his needs as important. Perhaps Congressman Polis, when looking for his next endeavor, could please visit the children who live in the Tobin, California district.

His alma mater, Princeton University, has excellent baseball and basketball summer camps. Perhaps he can select twelve boys and girls for the basketball camp and twelve more for the baseball camp whereby the children can live on the beautiful campus, receive healthy meals three times a day, be in a safe environment, and just might be inspired to aspire to a college education.

I always try to include a college campus visit on family vacations. When my daughter was ten, we went to Colonial Williamsburg and visited the campus of Hampton University in Virginia. She never forgot the beauty of Hampton U. Nine years later, she was accepted to Hampton and graduated four years after that with double honors. Sometimes a child needs to receive an experience, not more things.

Thank you Congressman Polis for demonstrating true leadership.

JANUARY 23RD

REFLECTIONS AT HOME
EXODUS 8: 20-32

THE IMPORTANCE OF LETTING GO

Is there a Pharaoh in your life?

The Egyptians and the Hebrews were two totally different and distinct cultures. The Hebrews were herdsman and led a nomadic lifestyle, while the Egyptians were more technology driven. The Hebrews were generally around animals all day which would give them a certain aroma as herdsmen and doers of animal sacrifices. Whereas the Egyptians led a lifestyle more intent on technology, the worship of certain animals, and luxurious baths and spas. Therefore, Pharaoh made the Hebrews live apart from the Egyptians, but not too far from his control.

Are you with someone who does not share your beliefs or value you?

To show his power, the Lord sent a plague of flies. Flies have no teeth and therefore consume only liquid food. In literature, when flies are mentioned, it is often a sign that death and decay are near. Being with the wrong person can suck the very life blood out of you causing a slow spiritual death and unfortunately sometimes a physical death. Flies only land on still targets.

"And the Lord said unto Moses, Rise up early in the morning and stand before Pharaoh . . . ." (Verse 20)

Pharaoh wanted a compromise. Have you heard, "It won't happen again" or "I'm sorry" more than once after a physical confrontation? Become an active member in the nearest church if you do not belong to one already. God will make a difference in your life IF you choose to make a difference. Moses walked a three-day journey into the wilderness to regain his way of life. How many more days will it take you to walk into your God-given destiny? First, pray to God for guidance and then pray with your pastor for the courage needed for your journey.

EGYPT
CARD #12

JANUARY 24TH

REFLECTIONS AT HOME
AMOS 6: 1-8

"WILLFUL BLINDNESS"

In law, the term "willful blindness" refers to a situation when someone sees an injustice of some kind, but makes a conscience decision to ignore it. This is the state we are currently in whereby ignorance, arrogance, and narcissism rule. No one remembered from their religious teachings that humility is the first sign of leadership. Amos warns that just attending church is not enough. In fact, the so-called Christians who are driven by greed and self-interest carry a greater guilt.

"Woe to them that are at ease in Zion . . ." (Verse 1)

"That lie upon beds of ivory,
And stretch themselves upon their couches . . ." (Verse 4)

When the current Supreme Court allowed big business to pour unlimited, undocumented wealth into the election process, they knew exactly what they were doing. There are those who will stop at nothing to defeat the first Black president of the United States. This is no different than the bribing of court officials referred to in verses 6 and 7. Judge Thomas and his wife have directly benefited from Supreme Court decisions, yet they see no conflict of interests.

-Research the facts and you decide.-

During the time of Amos, there did not exist a middle class. One was either very rich or very poor. Similar to today, if we allow the inaccurate sound bites of the newly elected Congress remain in Congress the fault is ours. It didn't seem as if any of them could explain what they were even voting on, like the debt ceiling. When did ignorance and lack of knowledge become acceptable?

Are you guilty of "willfil blindness"? No other President, anywhere near the academic accomplishments of President Obama, has had to endure the disrespect and lack of cooperation from those elected to represent ALL of the people. You have learned by now that Amos was given the mission to remind the wealthy not to exploit the poor nor profit from the downfall of others caused by the avarice of the wealthy. It is seen as a sin today just as it was in the day of Amos.

JANUARY 25TH

REFLECTIONS AT HOME
PROVERB 12: 22

OSCEOLA

"Lying lips are abomination to the Lord:
But they that deal truly are his delight."

All through school, it always amazed me how in textbook after textbook, we were told what the Indians had done to the White settlers. There was never any mention of what was done to the Indians except for a vague reference to The Trail of Tears. On October 21, 1837, General Thomas Sidney Jesup ordered the capture of Osceola. When the Seminole Indian arrived for the supposed truce negotiations at Fort Marion in Florida, he was immediately thrown in the brig. Under the harsh living conditions, Osceloa was dead by January of malaria.

Promise after promise was broken, yet there are some people today who claim that they have never been ashamed of our country. Whereas some of us learned of the Treaty of Moultrie Creek in 1823 where the Seminoles "gave" their land in Florida in return for a reservation, and the Treaty of New Echota in 1835 which removed the Cherokee off of their land. Some seem to have learned very little about the rich heritage of this diverse nation. In the Treaty of Payne's Landing of 1832, not only were the Florida Seminoles moved to Arkansas, but they were told to return all fugitive slaves now residing with them. Osceola had two wives, one of which was a Black woman.

When President Andrew Jackson signed the Indian Removal Act in 1830, he called for genocide. It's very sad that all of that suffering has been whitewashed by the undereducated representatives of today. It is important not to dwell on the atrocities of the 1800's, but it's just as important never to forget.

Using a semantic map (bicycle wheel) on the next page, write a five-paragraph essay with the title "Lying Lips." By using the map correctly, you will avoid redundancy (repeating yourself) and have a more organized piece. The more you practice, the better you become. It won't happen overnight.

Osceola

SEMANTIC MAPPING

Research the treaty made with each tribe. Write a general opening sentence about your topic. Then write five sentences about each tribe used on your information. Do not copy sentences from your research. Each new tribe is a separate paragraph. End with a paragraph giving your opinion.

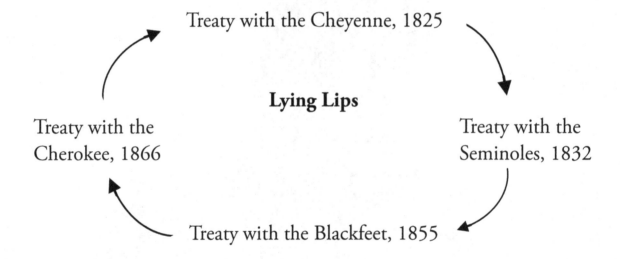

"Especially irksome are the Christians, who come and go everywhere as though theirs were the country . . . missionaries cause trouble everywhere. Their converts oppress those who do not wish to eat the foreign religion . . ."

From *Imperial Woman* by Pearl S. Buck

Always remember when trying to draw persons closer to God, not to completely destroy their culture in doing so. As they slowly learn the Word and see how you conduct yourself according to the teachings of Jesus, their idolatry will vanish. To convert, lead by example.

JANUARY 26TH

REFLECTIONS AT HOME
DEUTERONOMY 18: 9-14

PARADISE LOST

When is the last time you checked your horoscope? I think there are times when everyone wants a peek into the future, especially if it promises to be something positive, or something we want to hear like a new man or woman will be entering our life, or that we can expect a great deal of cash coming our way. As a whim or party ice-breaker, this can be entertaining. But, when a person feels that she cannot literally make a decision without first checking her horoscope, this falls into the realm of what Moses is warning about "practicing in the occult."

Moses goes on to say that God does not promise a trouble-free paradise. What he does promise is to not move the mountains, but to help you climb them. Many times, He places you in situations and locations because He wants you to make a difference. Our job is to be living witnesses to others, and to try and bring them closer to God's teachings.

One of the most beautiful places on Earth is Easter island located near Chile in South America. Before the onslaught of European slave traders in 1862, the Polynesian Aborigines flourished in the Rapa Nui culture, which included the Birdman Cult (research this). As customary, the healthiest individuals were captured and placed on slave ships and coupled with the European diseases brought by the mercenaries, the population dwindled.

To add insult to injury, next arrived the missionaries. As they had previously done in so many countries, they immediately began to destroy the culture of the natives.

". . . but as for thee, the Lord thy God hath not suffered thee so to do." (V 14) First, the dress was changed. Apparently only women who wear long sleeve garments will get into heaven. Then came the destruction of their culture. Body painting know as Takona art was banned as well as artworks, buildings, and the Rongo-rongo tablets which held the history of the Rapa Nui. As with the American Indian, they were forced off of their ancestral lands and required to live in one small section of the island. This is NOT how you bring people to God. They could not destroy the more that 650 elaborate petroglyphs (rock carvings)

What would Americans have done during WWII had it not been for the Navajo Code Talkers who confounded the Japanese by transmitting messages in their native language?

JANUARY 27TH

REFLECTIONS AT HOME
PROVERBS 21: 27

THE SACRISTAN vs THE SOLOIST

"The sacrifice of the wicked is an abomination;
How much more when he brings it with wicked intent!"

One of the most abominable things I have ever experienced is when our choir director was asked by a different pastor to come to his church to help his choir go from mediocre to excellent. They were good, but they had not mastered a few things that make the difference in a magnificent choir such as extended breathing, blending voices and keeping their eyes on the director and not buried in the music. After about a month, the director called a few of us who had been singing with him for over thirty years to come and sing with the new choir so they could hear what he was trying to teach. When we came (about six of us), we were met with animosity and were actually told, "We don't need you here". It was amazing that these so-called Christians were unknowingly such an abomination to the church. One Sunday a woman showed up who had not been to a rehearsal in over a month because someone had called and told her that someone else was going to sing "her" solo. Our maestro did not allow ownership of music nor did he allow anyone, divas included, to sing who had not come to rehearsals. She complained to the pastor, who then chastised the director.

What was the intent of the soloist? The Lord does not want such selfish sacrifices of giving your time and talents if it is done to glorify you and not Him. God cannot be bribed by outwardly insincere gestures of devotion to Him.

A beautiful place to visit if you ever travel to Argentina is called the Basilica de Nuestra Senora de Lujan at the end of the Plaza Belgrano. It took forty-eight years to build this cathedral (1887-1935), but its architecture which includes statues of the twelve disciples, fountains, and spires that seem to reach heaven is breath-taking. On the last Sunday of every September, a pilgrimage takes place when thousands of gauchos (cowboys) arrive on their horses to pay their respects to the Virgin. How the statue of the Virgin of Lujan finally made it to the place of the cathedral is a story I leave for you to research. Not only will you learn of the arduous task of her arrival but you will read the story of the slave, Manuel, who lived around 1677 and is now buried in a tomb at the foot of the altar. He was a sacristan whose motives and intent were to truly serve the Lord.

What is your motive for going to church?

JANUARY 28TH

REFLECTIONS AT HOME
DEUTERONOMY 25: 13-16

FAREWELL TO ONE WHO "BALANCED THE GRAIN"

Where can one find an honest man? Look no farther than to the Wisconsin Senator Kerb Kohl. Yes, the name sounds familiar because you probably have either shopped in the family business or watched his team, the Milwaukee Bucks, on television. During Senator Kohl's tenure in Congress, he has supported President Obama's Health Reform Legislation, is Pro Choice, Opposes the Death Penalty, and favors Affirmative Action for Minorities and Women. Because of his caring for those he has done business with, the Bible says that he will enjoy a long life. As a businessman, we know of his generosity. Senator Kohl gives annual grants to the University of Wisconsin-Madison; annual grants to 100 schools, 100 seniors, and 100 teachers. To those who much has been given, much is expected and Senator Kohl has certainly been the kind of man that pleases God.

As Senator Kohl retires next year, I ask that he visit Los Angeles Subdivision in Texas. They need your help. We know that the right man with the right heart can and will make a difference. You will be missed. Thank you.

When Senator Kohl leaves, who are we left with to handle the country's business? The likes of John Mica, the Chairman of the House Transportation and Infrastructure Committee. Yes, the name sounds familiar because he is one of the people responsible for shutting down the FAA. He is worth a cool 4.7 million, and does not have to use commercial airlines. With the abominable acts of John Mica, perhaps Jack Chagnon, the former teacher and Marine officer, who ran against John Mica and lost, is looking better and better to Floridians.

The Bible tells us that in business, always make sure to balance the grain—make even on both sides. Those representatives who cannot do this should be voted out and sent back home.

JANUARY 29TH

REFLECTIONS AT HOME
2 CORINTHIANS 3: 7-18

THE LIFTING OF THE VEIL

For some people, it is a struggle of belief between Christianity and Judaism, which is the religion of Jews, based on the teachings of Moses and the prophets as found in the Old Testament and on the interpretations of the rabbis who believe that the Messiah is still to come.

Throughout the Bible and even in the extended metaphor found in Shakespeare's Julius Caesar, when the veils were ripped during the crucifixion and murder, we no longer had to have a "middle-man" to talk to God. Moses wore a veil when he came back down Mt. Sinai with the Commandments to hide the radiance of his face. The veil illustrates the fading of the old system full of man-made laws and rituals that have nothing to do with eternal life with God. Why do people kiss the rings of men on Earth? Were not some of the disciples married? Removing the veil from your heart gives eternal life and as a mirror, you should reflect God's teachings. You no longer can be prideful and refuse to repent from your sins.

One of the most beautiful examples of the veil today is when a lovely bride walks down the aisle to the waiting arms of her future husband. When my daughter was married in the beautiful chapel at Hampton University with its stained glass ceiling, she really was a vision of beauty. Her face was absolutely radiant which could be seen behind her veil. As she was leaving the "old system" of me, myself, and I, she was walking into a new experience of sharing and caring. When you commit yourself in marriage, a moral transformation of the veil has to take place as well. There can no longer be selfishness and self-importance in a giving relationship. It can't always be about just you or your side of the family anymore. There is a Japanese saying that can be applied to both partners in marriage:

"No one before you, my husband

Not even I:

Remove the veil and live with God's new agreement in your heart.

HAMPTON U.
CARD #13

JANUARY 30ᵀᴴ

REFLECTIONS AT HOME
1 CORINTHIANS 15: 20-28

THOSE WHO HAVE FALLEN ASLEEP

Euphemism (yu fe miz em) is the use of a mild or indirect expression instead of one that is harsh. As we grow older and watch our parents walk a little slower, sleep a little more, and forget more often, we know that in the saga known as life, their days on Earth are drawing near an end. Usually, your mother will live longer than your father for various reasons (a younger age, in better health, etc). In the home, Dad was seen as the lion . . . strong, protective, and made you know that you were the center of his universe. But when your mother dies, no matter what age you are at the time of her death, an overwhelming sense of loneliness takes over your heart. For the first time in your life, you feel like an orphan, a little lost, a little frightened. Once they are buried, the ground in which they are asleep becomes sacred to you.

What makes the hallowed ground in Arlington or wherever your loved ones rest important? One of the most spiritual places on earth is Mt. Graham in Arizona. It is known to be the only place on earth with five climate zones as well as five species of trout living on the mountain. This mountain had been the hallowed ground of the Apache nation before the European immigrants and settlers came and made it a part of the San Carlos Reservation. As many times before, the federal government decided to "appropriate", or set aside this area and once again move the Apache in 1873.

Somehow this nation founded on those seeking religious freedom denied others the same freedom. In 1994, Congress passed riders to allow the University of Arizona to build a gigantic telescope on the summit. Today the Apaches organize the annual "protect run" up the mountain as a means to preserve their culture. As we read and study the Bible, we learn that "the last enemy that will be destroyed is death" in verse 26. Christ died and rose again as the firstfruit making a way for us to follow. The bodies of your loved ones may have been laid to rest at a beautiful, grassy location, but their spirit has overcome death.

CARD #14

JANUARY 31ST

REFLECTIONS AT HOME
ISAIAH 2: 10-22

THE OAK TREES OF BASHAN

Where is your "hiding place"?

During ancient times, people lived behind fortresses. Some consisted of high stone towers, or fortified walls with huge cisterns of hot oil as needed. Some hid in the limestone caves of Palestine. Even with extreme protection, we are told in these verses that man still has limitations. Throughout the Bible, man has proven to be unreliable and exhibit the tendency to worship objects. We are told in verse 20 to throw our gold and silver to the rats and bats for all the good it serves.

One of the 200 heathen gods worshiped by the Philistines was called Dagon, which was housed in a large temple known as E-Mul, or "House of the Star". King Saul's head was displayed in the temple of Dagon (1 Chronicles 10). Fake gods will be responsible for providing whatever the need is in a particular location. Therefore, Dagon is known as the "fish-god" or god of grains. The Lord God is omnipresent and cannot be confined to man-made walls no matter the grandeur of such. The Lord God will supply all of your needs, not just your physical hunger. Do you hide at home, making excuses why you can't come out? Have you done something so terrible that you live in fear that one day your secret will be a secret no longer?

The land of Bashan, east of the Jordan River, was called the "bread basket of the world". Bashan was also known for its oak trees. Oak is heavy and hard, strong and beautiful, and supplies food. With sustenance, one is strong and fearless. With trees, one has shade and shelter. God wants us to apply His teachings to our lives and not be short-sighted by worshiping the various cults of the day. Like oak tress, we are to stand firm in our beliefs, and be strong in our commitment. He will shelter you from harm and when you believe this, there is no reason to hide anymore.

The Lord has always been a refuge for me in the time of storm and has blessed me mightily. After delivering my son, the nurse brought him to me all cleaned up and pink and as she handed him to me, she said what should we call him? He stretched out his little hand and grabbed my finger and gazed at me with his curious grey eyes, and I said, "Call him Bashan."

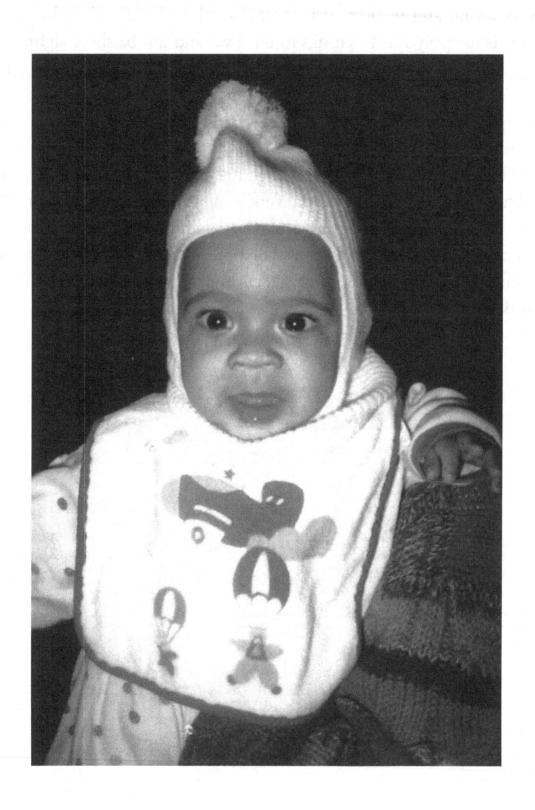

DESCRIPTIVE WRITING

When you were taught to write in elementary school, you probably were drilled on the beginning, the body, and the ending and the use of transitional words (therefore, and, whereas, etc.) to help expand the length of your sentences. Too often, that's as far as many students get.

When you take the college board exam, you must demonstrate literary skills, knowledge of literary terminology, and reference skills. Students are not born as "poor test-takers". It's sometimes the lack of having ever mastered the basics, second-class schools, and third-rate teachers.

Draw the following: a huge eel

DESCRIPTIVE WRITING

Now draw a huge eel with fangs, tentacles all over its body with claws on the end of two of them, and six spiraling tentacles around its mouth.

Do you see the difference when you add some adjectives. You want the reader to visualize your ideas. Example: She had long, black hair. (not good enough) She had long, thick, glossy black hair that caressed the curves of her hips as she leisurely sauntered across the school cafeteria. (better)

WHAT I NOW KNOW

1. How would you describe the ministry of Amos?

2. Three of the most impoverished places in the United States are in Texas. Where?

3. Name five of the six millionaire Congress people mentioned.

4. Name one of the novels mentioned that you read.

5. What is situational irony?

6. What is the difference between a vision and a dream?

7. Name 2 of the 6 things mentioned in Proverbs that the Lord hates.

JANUARY

REFLECTIONS AT HOME
KNOWLEDGE IS POWER

Vocabulary Enhancement & Family Activities

1. Kumsan = a long cotton shirt reaching to the ankles and gathered at the waist with a wide sash, worn by men in Morocco, N. Africa (have your teens make these and place designs on the back using sequins; puff paints; etc.)
2. Kojah = a mutant variety of mink (have your little ones draw a picture of this "stinky" mink after they look it up & write a poem about it)
3. Knock down-drag-out = hand-to-hand combat (movie & pop-corn night watching kung-fu)
4. Knarl = a knot on a tree in wood (plant a dwarf fruit tree in the Fall)
5. Kirundi = a Bantu language of Burundi, a country in eastern central Africa (draw a map of Burundi *by hand* and its surrounding countries) Teach your children that Africa is a continent with many countries; have the older siblings watch the movie *Hotel Rwanda*

Family Nigerian Dinner: Each individual fixes one dish
(find recipes on the internet)

—chicken curry
—grilled fish
—pineapple crumble

—coconut fried rice
—shrimp kabobs
—sliced mangoes

—black-eyed peas   —yams
—egusi stew   —akara cakes (pancakes)

Reading Corner: *Everything Good Will Come* by Sefi Atti
         Found at www.amazon.com
         (excellent for those who wish to have a career in civil rights)

GREETING CARDS
(Blank on the inside)

ALL CARDS ARE IN COLOR AND MAY BE ORDERED ONLINE BY CONTACTING:
zoftig2@comcast.net

Single cards are $2.50 plus tax
Box of 12 of your choice is $20.00 plus tax